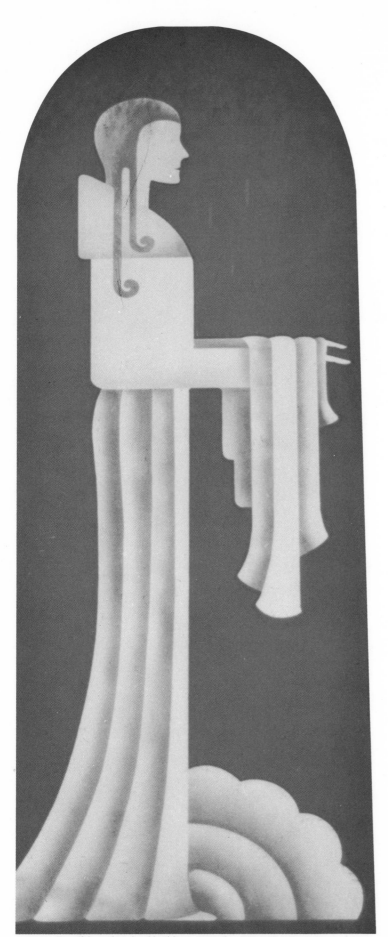

*Detail from facade of building on Market Street, San Francisco;*
*photograph by Gigi Carroll, San Francisco.*

# ART DECO

## JOHN HULL

## TROUBADOR PRESS

*Detailed from facade mosaic by Gerald Fitzgerald for the Paramount Theatre, Oakland; photographed by Cathe Centorbe, San Francisco.*

## Troubador DESIGN RESOURCE Series

The Design Resource Series provides graphic references and design motifs with photographs, illustrations, and patterns ready to use. The illustrations in this book may be reproduced on any non-commercial project for home or classroom, free and without special permission. Include a credit line indicating the book title and publisher. Write the publisher for permission to make more extensive use of the materials in the book or for commercial purposes. The republication of this book in whole or in part beyond the specifications above is prohibited.

### Library of Congress Cataloging in Publication Data

Hull, John, 1942—
    Art Deco : design motifs of the 20's & 30's.

    (Design resource series)
    1. Decoration and ornament — Art deco.   2. Art industries and trade.
I. Title.
NK789.5.A7H84          709'.04          75-37604
ISBN 0-912300-62-0

# CONTENTS

*Top:* The Big Breakfast *by Fernand Léger, 1921. Bottom left: 1925 painting of the Eiffel Tower by Robert Delaunay, an early cubist. Bottom right: detail of cubist* Portrait of D. H. Kahnweiler *by Pablo Picasso, 1910.*

*The entrance to the Pharaoh Apartment House, above left, is an excellent example of the Egyptian influence on Art Deco. Photo: Gigi Carroll, San Francisco. Above right: small gold mummiform coffin from the tomb of Tutankhamen.*

# INTRODUCTION

Art Deco is a decorative style that emerged in the nineteen-twenties and became internationally popular. It reached its most widespread acceptance in the thirties and developed into the Streamline Style of the forties.

Designers and artists of the twenties and thirties were fascinated by the developing technology of industry. The artists attempted to unite industry with art by using factory imagery in their work, and the designers put the new technical knowledge into practice on items for industrial manufacture. The repetition of shapes in Art Deco designs, particularly mechanical shapes made with compasses, triangles and straight edges, is an example of mass production methods applied to design.

There were several other influences on Art Deco. The style made its first appearance in the world of fashion in the early twenties. Parisian designers were excited to experiment with new color combinations — orange and green, purple and scarlet — by the Leon Bakst designs for the Russian Ballet.

Decoists were also inspired by the International Style of Design, with its emphasis on functionalism propounded by the de Stijl group in the

*On the left:* The Girl and the Penguins *by Edgar Walter, from the "Court of Reflections" at the 1939 Golden Gate International Exposition on San Francisco's Treasure Island. Right top: a relief sculpture by Jacques Schnier from Berkeley High School; photo by Gigi Carroll, San Francisco. Right bottom: the Empire State Building, long the world's tallest building.*

Netherlands and the Bauhaus School in Germany, where designers such as Gropius and Albers attempted to create a "better" world through a consistent design philosophy. From them, designers adopted the clean circular and rectilinear shapes that became typical of Art Deco.

King Tut's tomb was opened in 1923 and suddenly Egyptiana was the rage. This, with Middle Eastern and Pan-American archeological influences, explains the importance of ziggurat, or stepped pyramid shapes, in Art. Deco.

The Decoists were also greatly effected by developments in the fine arts, particularly Cubism. The jagged angular shapes of Cubist painters such as Braque and Picasso were quickly incorporated into the developing Deco style.

Art Deco is distinguished by geometric shapes and patterns, diagonals, spirals, zig-zags, symmetry, visual progressions, repetitions and particular recurrent subject themes. The latter include animals and women, often shown together, stylized flowers and foliage, lightning flashes and suns-with-rays. Speed and motion — depicted by dancing figures, moving trains, boats, planes, cars and running animals, especially dogs and deer — are also characteristic.

The skyscraper epitomized Art Deco architecture. The new technology made taller structures possible, while building zone laws dictated that the width of buildings decrease by set amounts as the height increased. This resulted in the typical "stepped-back" look of Art Deco skyscrapers.

The sculpture of the period often has an Art Deco look also, and relief sculpture in cement or plaster was extensively employed for both expressive and decorative purposes.

It is easy to appreciate the great visual elegance and excitement of the period. This book contains contemporary craft projects using design motifs in the Art Deco style. As you develop a feeling for Art Deco, your projects will have the clean fresh look that makes the style persistently appealing.

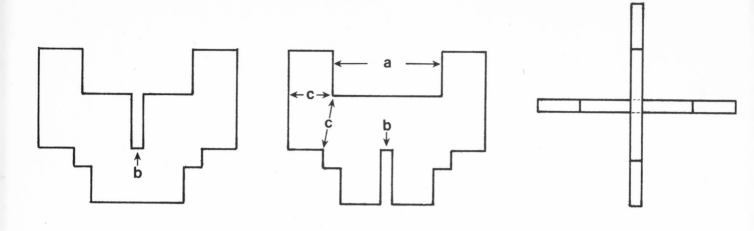

# WOODWORKING

Design and build your own hanging plant holder. Start with the silhouette of your pot and saucer. The widest point becomes the width of cutout 'a'. The thickness of your wood becomes the width of the 'b' cutouts. The 'c' widths should be good and wide because these are the weakest stress points. The outside shape can be as you like it. Construct a variation on the ziggurat or stepped design — popular during the Art Deco period — seen in the clock at left. Cut out 2 pieces as shown above left and center. Paint on a couple of Deco stripes and slot them together as shown in the top view, above right. Now it's a tabletop plant holder. Add screw eyes and cords to hang. Clock courtesy of Robert Thompson, Northfield, Minneapolis.

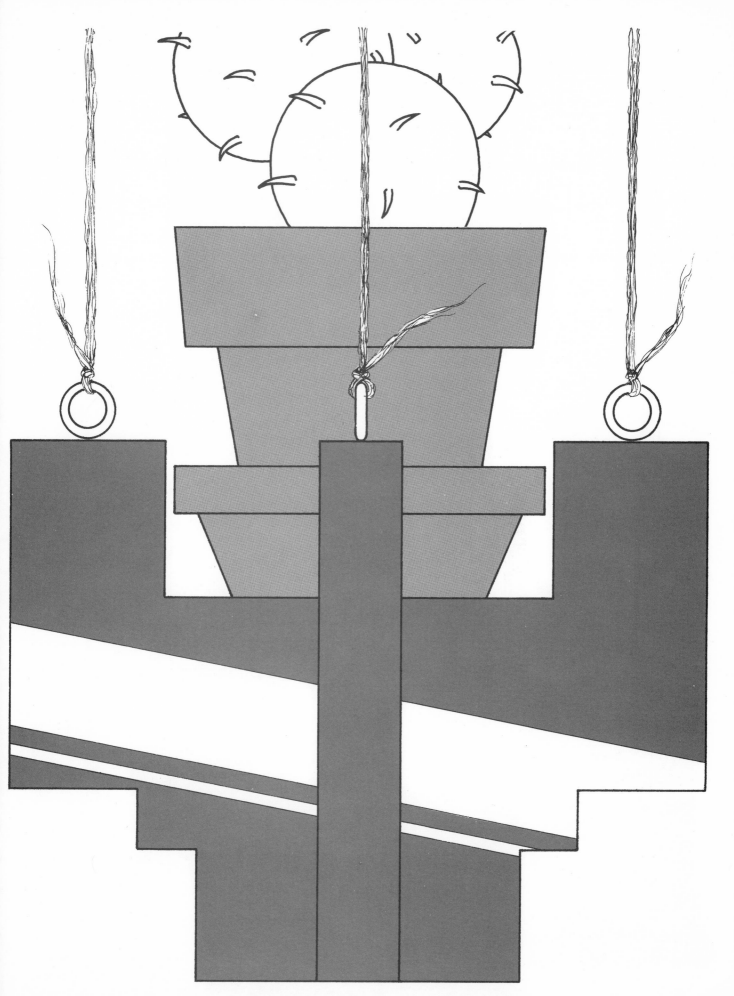

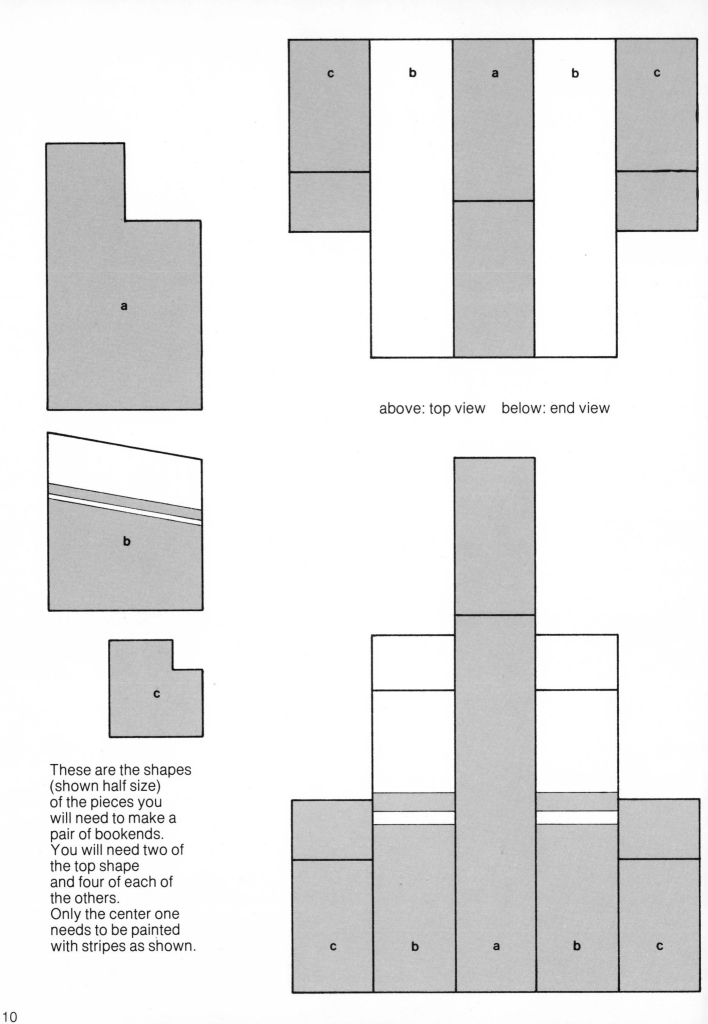

above: top view    below: end view

These are the shapes
(shown half size)
of the pieces you
will need to make a
pair of bookends.
You will need two of
the top shape
and four of each of
the others.
Only the center one
needs to be painted
with stripes as shown.

Make bookends to coordinate with the plant holder.
Cut out the pieces as explained at the far left.
Paint them and glue together as shown in the top
and end views shown at the left.

below: side view

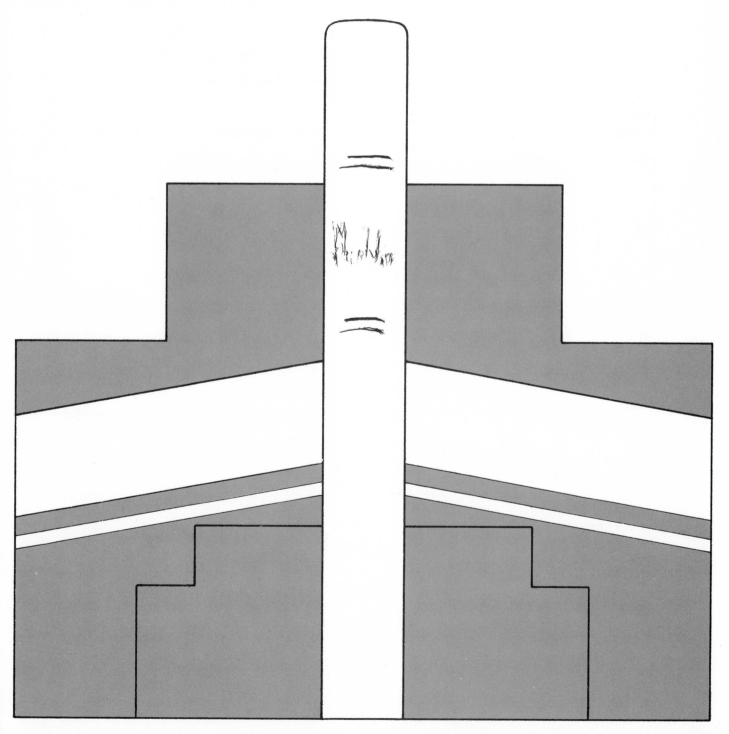

# CERAMICS

Both the form and decoration of the vases on the right and on page 14 typify Art Deco. The geometric cactus-like shapes in the example of Red Wing Pottery above, photographed by Gigi Carroll of San Francisco, are also characteristic of Art Deco. The double vase is a light natural color with the figure's dress glazed to contrast. Courtesy of Robert Loughlin, Flying "A" Service, San Francisco.

*Design for a vase
adapted from a piece of
enameled porcelain Carlton Ware,
English, c. 1925.*

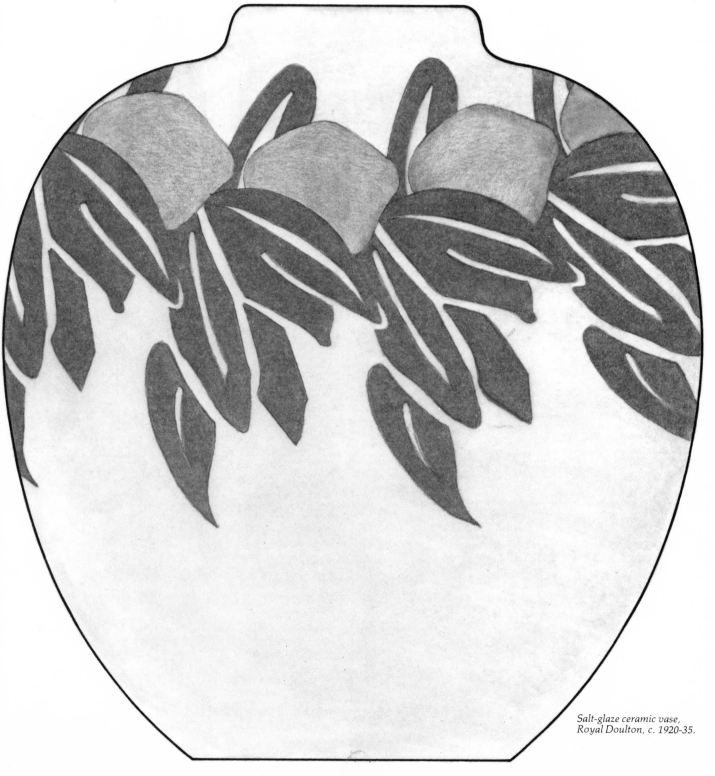

*Salt-glaze ceramic vase,
Royal Doulton, c. 1920-35.*

# LEATHERWORK

Make a tooled and dyed leather shoulder bag and wallet as pictured on the right and above. The photograph at the left shows a detail of a cement relief decoration from a building entrance on Folsom Street in San Francisco. Its design can be easily adapted for a tooled leather belt. The geometric pattern shown at the top of the page provides another Deco belt design.

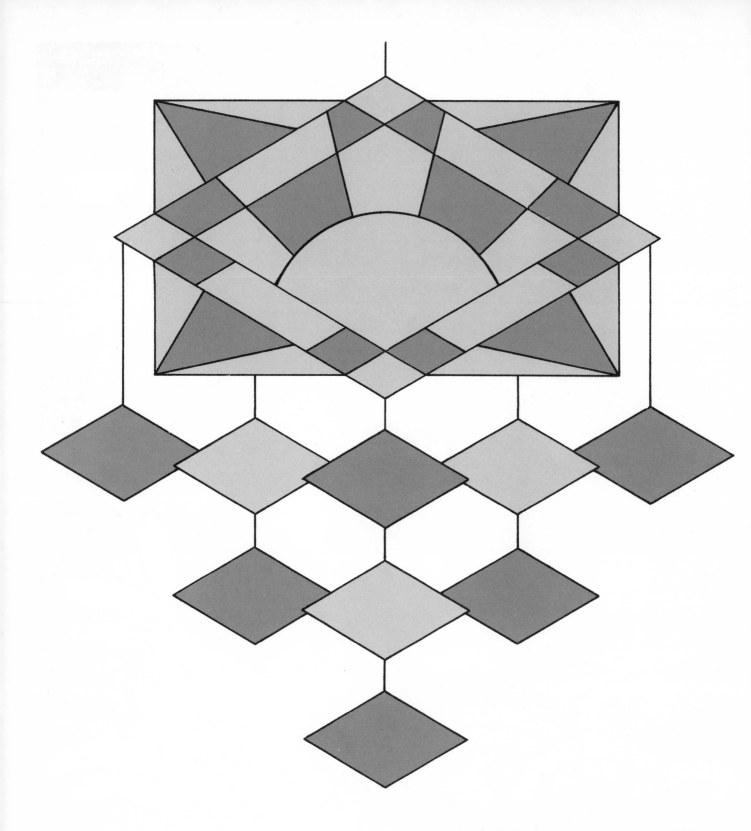

# STAINED GLASS

For an unusual Art Deco stained glass project, make the wind chime shown above or the window on the right. This window, entitled "Twilight," is from a design by J. Gaudin after a sketch by L. Mazetier. Considering the subject, cool "evening" colors such as blues, greens and purples would be appropriate.

The still life below and the figurative design on the
right are from a stained glass window by
J. Gaudin, after a design by Elesz Kiervicz, for a
restaurant. You may add the still life to the bottom
of the design opposite for a longer,
narrower composition.

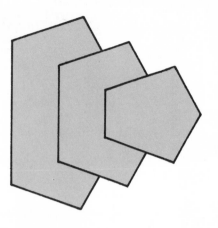

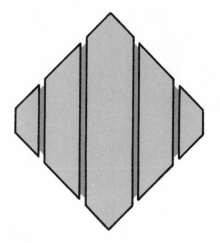

# JEWELRY

An example of the strongly geometric design dominant in Art Deco can be seen above in the Czechoslovakian etched crystal perfume bottles, c. 1935. The atomizer bulb ends in an elegant tassel in these superb examples of Art Deco from the Stephen Wirtz Gallery in San Francisco, photographed by Gigi Carroll. Create your own Art Deco pins or belt buckles using the designs shown on the tops of these pages, or make a necklace or bracelet as pictured at the center and lower right. The necklace is from a design by Raymond Templier.

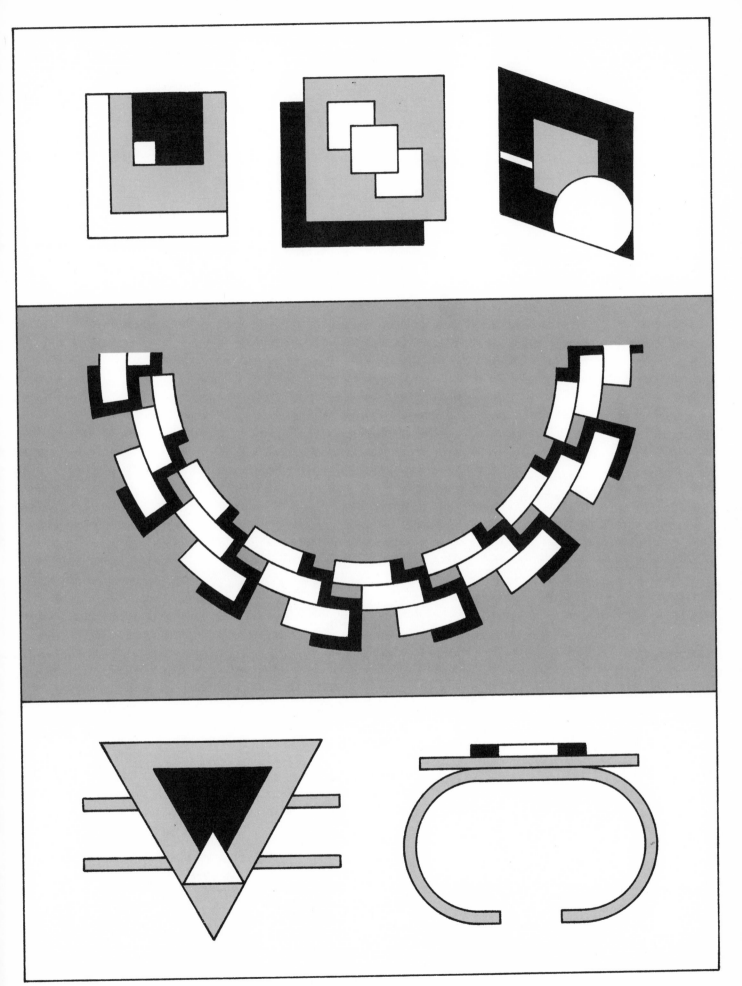

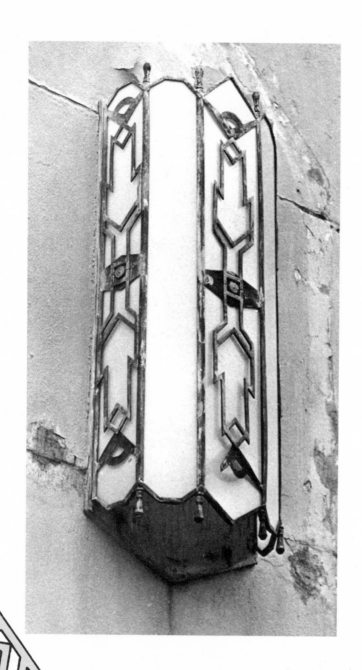

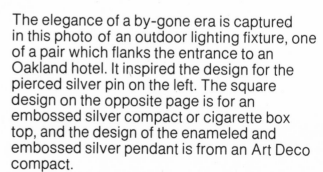

The elegance of a by-gone era is captured in this photo of an outdoor lighting fixture, one of a pair which flanks the entrance to an Oakland hotel. It inspired the design for the pierced silver pin on the left. The square design on the opposite page is for an embossed silver compact or cigarette box top, and the design of the enameled and embossed silver pendant is from an Art Deco compact.

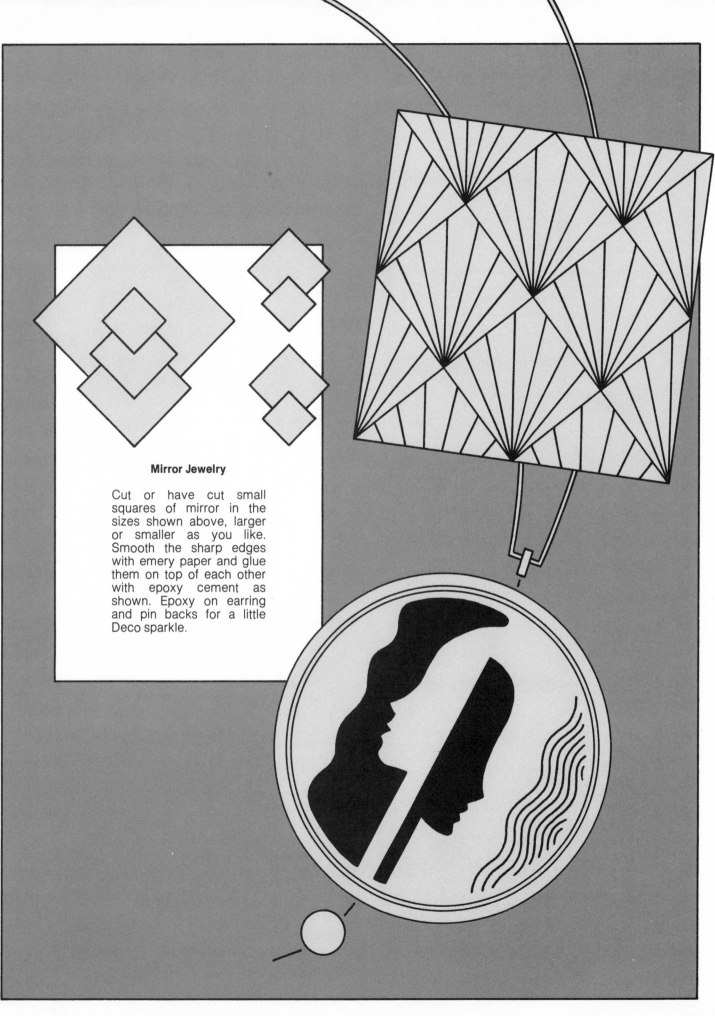

### Mirror Jewelry

Cut or have cut small squares of mirror in the sizes shown above, larger or smaller as you like. Smooth the sharp edges with emery paper and glue them on top of each other with epoxy cement as shown. Epoxy on earring and pin backs for a little Deco sparkle.

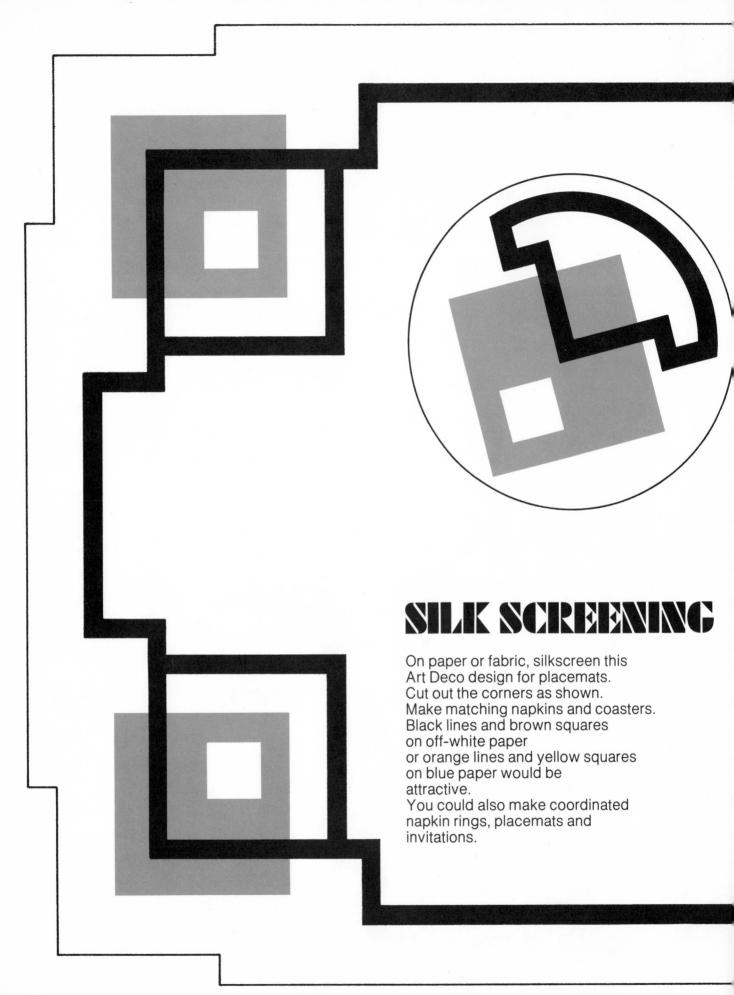

# SILK SCREENING

On paper or fabric, silkscreen this
Art Deco design for placemats.
Cut out the corners as shown.
Make matching napkins and coasters.
Black lines and brown squares
on off-white paper
or orange lines and yellow squares
on blue paper would be
attractive.
You could also make coordinated
napkin rings, placemats and
invitations.

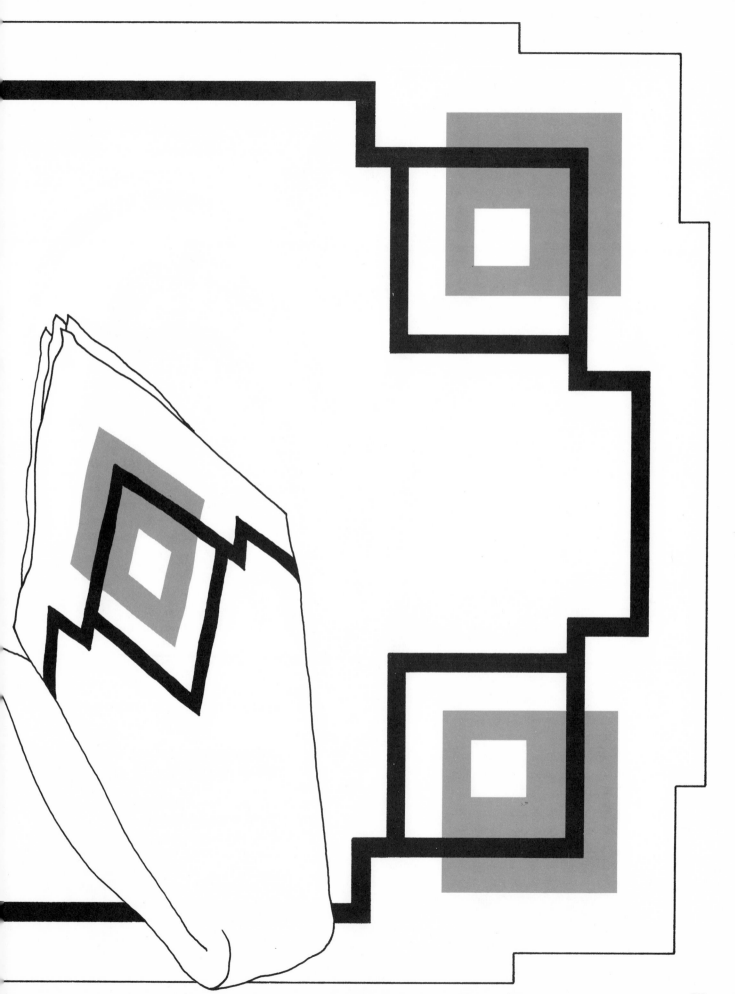

# STENCILING

The settee and wall panel from the women's lounge in the Paramount Theatre in Oakland are detailed from a photograph by Steven Levin of San Francisco. The flower motif above is adapted for stenciling from this wall decoration. The center circle of the flower will have to be a separate stencil, since it is not connected to the outside edge of the design. On the right: stencils for a border pattern and for a sunrise at sea.

# GRAPHICS

Above appears a poster advertising soap, designed by Jupp Wiertz in 1927, and shown on the right, from the same year, is a poster by Guaro for a French resort. The man hurrying to catch a train was found on a poster by Austin Cooper for the London & North Eastern Railway. It demonstrates how Art Deco designers typically depicted speed and motion by using repetition of a shape with a progression of tones.

# Broadway

## ABCDEFGHIJKL MNOPQRSTUVWXYZ abcdefghijklm nopqrstuvwxyz

# Futura

## ABCDEFGHIJKLM NOPQRSTUVWXYZ abcdefghijkl mnopqrstuvwxyz

Broadway and Futura are the two most typical Art Deco typefaces. Paul Renner designed Futura in 1927 according to the strict geometry of the International Design Movement, which was also an important element of Art Deco. Broadway survives as a popular display face, along with the many delightful variations it inspired.

The border design of waves and fishes below is adapted from a motif by Bob Howard, which appears in gilt relief, decorating the area above the proscenium in the Paramount Theatre in Oakland.

Create a "shaped-canvas" painting of your
initial by enlarging the appropriate letter
from the alphabet which begins above.
Cut the silhouette of the letter out of board
and paint the design as desired.

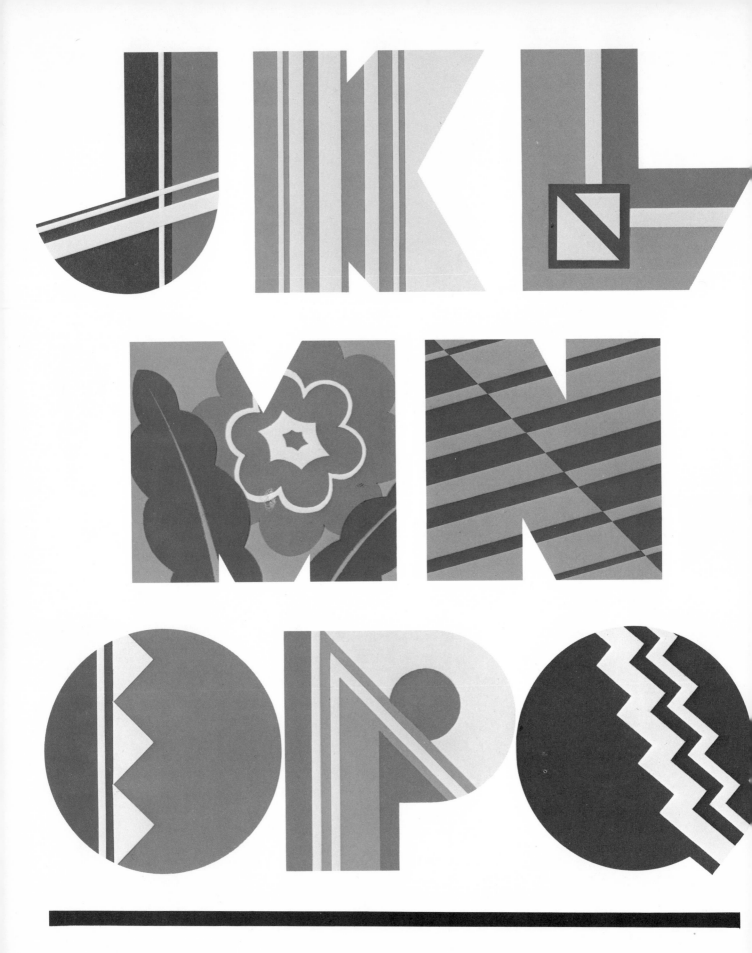

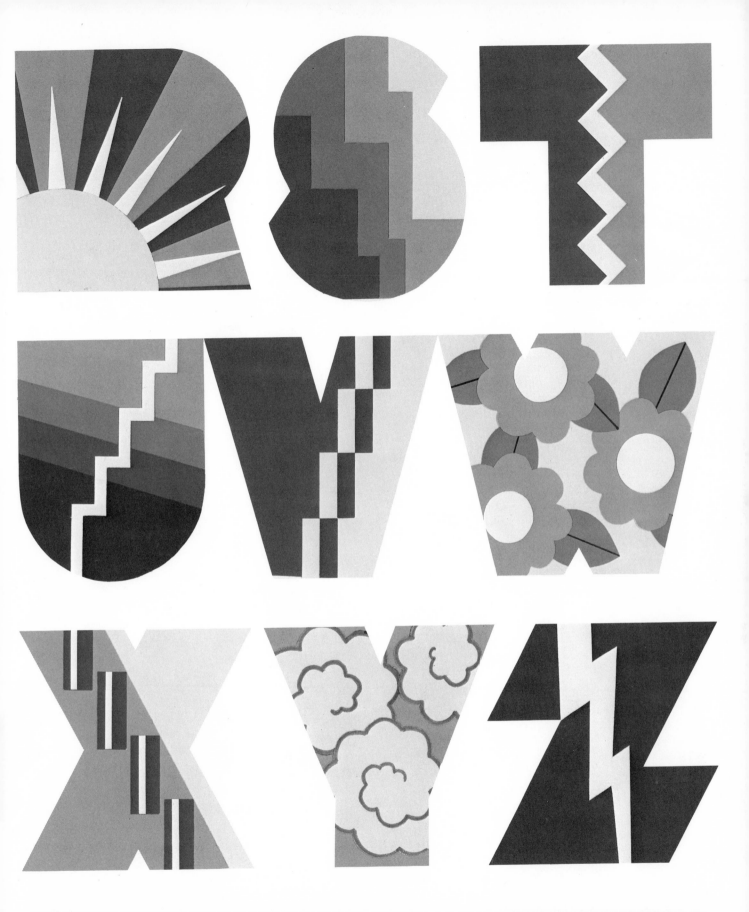

# PAINTING AND DECORATION

The drawing of a deer among stylized flowers is from an English Poole Pottery wall plate design, c. 1925. It can easily be enlarged and transferred to a canvas or panel. Paint the line work in blue and fill in with greens, yellows and purples, shading the deer with tawny beige and white, to approximate the original Deco coloring.

The photograph shows a bronze lamp base with a gazelle and crescent motif, courtesy of Robert Thompson, Northfield, Minneapolis.

This photograph of a sofa, end tables and
lamps ensemble from the Paramount Theatre in
Oakland is by Cathe Centorbe. The Paramount is a
completely restored Art Deco Movie Palace, now the
home of the Oakland Symphony Orchestra.
All the Deco excitement is as it was during the thirties,
providing a marvelous example of not just a
single element, but a totality of
Art Deco decoration.

Your own Art Deco lamps can be much simpler,
as shown at the right. Slipcover a table lamp with a
decorated cylinder of heavy silvered paper and
decorate a straight sided lamp shade to go with it.

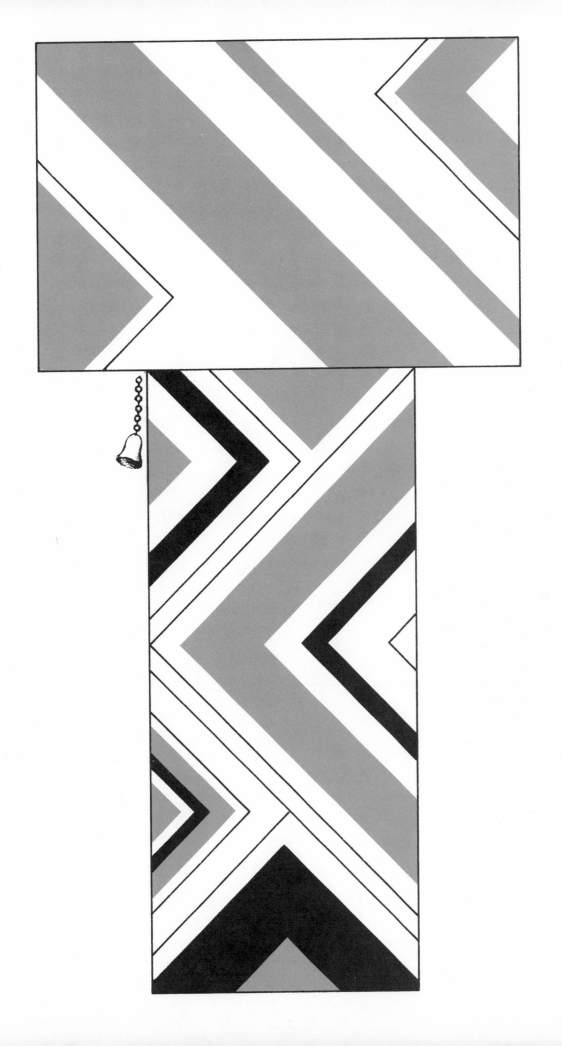

# QUILTING

Make an Art Deco quilt. Work out your colors in the line drawing opposite, using the illustration above to know where colors repeat. Substitute a pattern — especially one with a period feeling — for one of the solids. From a design by Pierre Legrain.

# WEAVING AND RUG MAKING

The design above is from a flat woven rug by Sonia Delaunay. It could also be used as a wall hanging. Warm oranges and browns with white and dark grey would be good colors to use. The design on the right is for a short pile knotted or hooked rug.

43

# NEEDLEWORK

Embroider or applique a necktie or a pair of gloves for a little Deco excitement. The rectangular design could be used for a needlepoint clutch purse for those special evenings out, or larger, for a striking needlepoint pillow, colored in brown and white. The flower motifs could be embroidered or appliqued onto a blouse, a skirt, a blazer or a pair of jeans.

**Fashions to sew in Art Deco**

*Made in pretty soft fabrics, these stiff fashion fantasies will come alive with moving curves.*

*left to right*

*peach and white crocheted breakfast robe that buttons once on the hip*

*for checking the stables, the hives, the kennels, the gardens, and ordering the car, a 4-pocket work suit*

*for mornings at the track, a meeting, café with a friend, adapted from Harper's Bazaar*

figure and
dress
based on
a design by
Erté,
an early genius
of Art Deco

scarlet,
black and
jade
tea gown

black and
silver
evening gown

I would like to thank Malcolm Whyte, Kent Tichenor, Brenda Shahan, Helena Virtanen and Mylo Schaaf of Troubador Press, Ellen Dietschy, Ruth Cravath, Anne Breckenridge, Ann Bailey, Tom Hughes, Marc Arceneaux, Alfred Bauman,

*Decorative lamp courtesy of Cork Marcheschi, Minneapolis, Minnesota.*

Tommy Luken, Zephyr Rocket, Inc., and the photographer Bruce Sheffler in St. Paul, Jim Rivaldo and all my friends at Blue Print Service Company, Copy Service and Lin Litho.

John Hull